what the auntys say

what the auntys say

Sharron Proulx-Turner

McGilligan Books

National Library of Canada Cataloguing in Publication

Proulx-Turner, Sharron
        What the auntys say / Sharron Proulx-Turner.
Poem.
ISBN 1-894692-04-77
        1. Métis—Poetry. I. Title.

PS8581.R68983W46 2002   C811'.6   C2002-903488-4
PR9199.4.P76W46 2002

Versions of some of these poems have appeared in *absinthe magazine* and in
Gatherings: The En'owkin Journal of First North American Peoples.

Editor: Weyman Chan
Copy editor: Noreen Shanahan
Interior design: Heather Guylar
Author photo: Joy Hendrickson
Cover design: Heather Guylar

McGilligan Books gratefully acknowledges the support of The Canada Council for
the Arts, the Ontario Arts Council and the Ontario Book Publisher Tax Credit for
our publishing program.

ONTARIO ARTS COUNCIL
CONSEIL DES ARTS DE L'ONTARIO

THE CANADA COUNCIL | LE CONSEIL DES ARTS
FOR THE ARTS | DU CANADA
SINCE 1957 | DEPUIS 1957

Acknowledgments

I would like to offer my deep gratitude to the great spirit, to my grand-mothers and grandfathers and my family and friends who have given me the spiritual and emotional support and encouragement to tell these stories: my grandmothers exilda dufort, rosina lafrance, anna lafrance, germaine proulx, lillianne proulx, josephte larocque, catherine brazeau, louise durocher, marie pinel de la chaunaie, cecile groulx, anne julienne dumont, elizabeth trottier; my mother, joan boyce and her sisters, the twins, cathy and especially evelyn, without whom the auntys and the old lady in these stories would have remained thought-memories; aruna srivastava for your beautiful you; lucy and camille russell for being the parents I never had; my kids my teachers, graham and barbra and adrian; my grandkids monica, willow and baby jessinia, for your wonderlove; my sister joy for your many miracles; amina dawed-baker for your sisterlove; chris goodwin, river-spirit woman, for your youth and brilliance; shirley bear, my life-long hero; ashok mathur for your love and weeks of amazing editing space; weyman chan for your friend-ship and editing skills extraordinaire; renee lang, rhonda west, joe white, kitti freeman, cheach riesen, margie lee, fritz bitz, donna mcphee, kym hines, naomi north, lori wildcat, hiromi goto, jesse brazeau, jim bazant, gladys srivastava, alice lee, mayumi futamura, edna and george blondeau, jordan bruised head, morris crow, geoff burtonshaw, jillian good eagle a.k.a. dr. wolf collar, for believing in me and giving so much of yourselves; rita joe, maria campbell, beatrice mosionier, buffy sainte-marie, phyllis webb, beth brant, luce irigary, daniel david moses, richard van camp, lee maracle, louise halfe, toni morrison, jeannette armstrong, chrystos, audre lorde, paula gunn allen, joy harjo, joanne arnott, for wording your way into me.

special thanks to the creative writing folks at the university of calgary: fred wah, who is among the great teachers and critics; aritha van herk for your unmatched energy and encouragement; chris wiseman for your exactness; canada council for the arts and the alberta foundation for the arts for providing me with uninterrupted writing time.

finally, ann decter, heather guylar and noreen shanahan at mcgilligan books, thank you so much for doing absolutely everything I would have asked of you without even having to ask; and to the family and friends I haven't mentioned here, know that I wouldn't be the person I am without you in my life.

with deep love
I dedicate these stories
in memory of
mazie cunningham-mcphee

Contents

we are the auntys and these are our voices as told to our girl
we tell her you are a poet you've got the gift you tell these
  stories
about your women your children
you weave these stories into one long birth of one old metisse
  lady
just before and after the indian act
outlawed seven generations hidden inside raw deep pain a
  shame
so pure
the white man makes us illegal forces us into his churches his
  towns
takes our babes our boys our girls
generation after generation

you show our children our past our unawares
we live our grandmothers' lives over and over
same old stereotypes same old lines
woven through our stories
vicious circles through time

yet here we are we tell our girl
and now is our time
our time to remember our time to heal
same spirit guides
same four directions
same great spirit

we tell her our voice is preachy tone us down
but only some where we come from
politics and poetry sit in the same circle talk the same line

metisse means metis woman-girl
two bloods not half and half like cream

a nation of our own the metis nation
we teach we learn from the old ones the elders who tell us

honour the blood of both our mothers
and our fathers
we make the balance
we are neither
native nor non-native

we are both
where bannock or scone or cornbread
known by many names
still tastes like a dream come true

in first peoples country
where to look too much like a white person
means good first people turn their backs to you
at sweat lodge and ceremonies passing

judgment thinking you must be a white a wannabee
in first peoples country
where to look too much like a first peoples person
means no pow wow trail for you
don't even know who your people are must be an apple a
    wannabee
in first peoples country
quantumed just like old macdonald indian agent still makes the
    rules

these days unless you go to hollywood
you got the metis nation plague

in white man country
some got metis cards

14

many are turned away by our metis leaders
young men who are not yet grandfathers
won't bend as if scrip determines who's metis
or greedy for that little bit of land
and where did those red river metis come from
those weren't no white men
already three hundred years of two bloods who migrated
from the east

and what about the ones who stayed behind
that's our kind   us auntys
we metis we're scattered here and there not yet the one great
*   nation*
we're meant to be

some learn traditional ways and pray to the great spirit
some go to church and pray to god
some turn their backs on prayer
some jig it's true some fiddle too some like poetry some like
to party hard
some speak the michif cradle tongue
verbs are cree ojibwe nouns french english
most speak english or french some speak other languages too

we tell our girl
your children carry the seventh generation of this story
a story of growth and pain and a nation birthing out from an
unfamiliar egg
an egg a world where your children are not welcome on either
*   side*
the native or the non-native
to one side to the other a fence they didn't build
belly shame and deep deep pain on both sides

tell this story this way my girl
the way you're taught to pray each moment of the day
there's a lesson in every rock every leaf every ivory tower
and this is how our story goes

part i
a few eggs short of a picnic

and crow is serving rainbows to the stars

as this story goes
grows sixteen generations many first peoples deep
these are metisse women backbone of the land
teachers doctors lawyers farmers
midwives medicine women mothers girls
their men the courier du bois voyageurs
farmers trappers hunters warriors
in the olden times
to this day their children shamed on both sides

a day or two away
light like sun comes up and through the ground
wide and round
a hole and not a hole
light like moon on water
bees hover near the top
and out climbs that old lady

roots and medicines scrabble chess and shopping carts
her metis sash tight around her waist

reaches for her walking stick
black cherry cut with fine white pine
and gentle curve of crow
so real
so blue

they thought she'd died of a heart attack

stuffs that white powder in her mouth all on her own   eating at
those fine white lines between the black scribbles   noisy painful
death   her nighty up around her face to keep those eyes from
gawking   at her shame

her pain her anger shows   around her heart and all her life shows
tells how   over and over   and her heart bursts out to scratches
wasted on the page

they thought she'd died when the tear gas they threw at her and
the kids
backfires
on account of the pulp mill fumes uranium acid rain
this is just before the whitetown cop trips over his dog
and submachineguns
the united nations rapporteurs
whose western wear can now be seen
in the indian section
over at whitetown museum

they say she looked like life brown ground
sparse grass blowing around and on itself
bright daylight soft warm air
she sure didn't take up too much space
is what the auntys say
and all she ever wanted was to love
someones like herself
intense
intelligent
kind

they thought she'd died of a heart attack
murmur the size of a scream
the pain of hearing
resting clinging
to her salt

circle after circle says the sun that hot round day warms words too
hard to bite and chew like jawbreakers

suck the layers feel each one
I am many things says the old lady
but I am no dentist chair
I can pee in the snow with the best of them

they thought she'd died in an open vat
blue dye from them jawbrakers all in her hair her skin her eyes
wide open

22

it was all a dream they said
no one no woman not even a stuffed doll could say
how or why she died
touch touch her hands between her palms   died
so much love all that love
there's no way to know only
speculation never expected to carry   died

heavy salted strangers in their robes
they say she was murdered right there where she slept   died

snuggle struggle knotted hair
her braid gone makes it quick
she's having heart trouble
had it only a week and already it's broken down
they were right all along those auntys
wording those feelings
well you certainly need a car these days
to colour in that circle

truth is she was just too busy to die
gives and loves and lives
three maybe four hundred years
is what the auntys say
tells them robed ones go stuff themselves
saves the babys saves the kids
kids animals birds and all the plants
even the fish and water ones
at night you can see her
standing glowing the air around her
salty with a view

and there's them eggs talking
under the breath of a new cottonwood
even and
arms full of kindle
waiting to burn

when crows are big as airplanes

it is said if you can talk you can sing
and if you can walk you can dance
and you must
trust

first song sung by that old lady comes to her in a dream   is what
the auntys say   empty eggs all greenyblue outrageous   and out
bursts whitetown in the middle of the day

young crow or raven nuzzles deep into her spine
kicks up a heel-toe dance
opposite the sun
sings indian and white the mix is just right
indian and white the mix is just right
while the old lady offers kinikinik
her love her thanks for life this song and all creation
right up from inside the round
of mother earth and weeping of days
creator I'm reaching out to you
her tears and fears and faces east

15

that's when her thoughts birth whitetown
soft as rain and south of space or time
full and candy sweet
a grief whose face is fire
loud and quiet
utter love

pain is not egg-shaped
which is why you'll hear that old lady's song
just to left and in the middle
of your right brain
lyrical and long
is what the auntys say
washing dishes in an electric storm
out the back window there'll be houses
crowded together
flames suckling on the wind
hands limp and hanging
from the line
still hasn't shed a tear for fear she'll wander
past belief
fingers curled in fingers
eyes in eyes

they say that old lady used to spend lots of time trailing waiting
praying for a miracle   and out pops this big red hen body the size of
a car   one of them volkswagens except with chicken scratches on
the road   and in hops the old lady ties a scarf around her hair and
gets behind the wheel   the whole time up front in the trunk of that
car them eggs   birthed blind

whisper she is magic she is ready to return remember
she is magic she is ready to return

this is way back before tv was even a pimple on a newborn's butt
good shocks on that car burden of the past
inside long grass or water
and pulling into tide
shadowed by a whitetown crowd
where hundreds and hundreds of gulls
hover
shrill-hunger wailing
to a round and open wind
west pushes from inside
young birds whose sightless eyes
clear water poisoned
meet her own

there's where there's folks from whitetown
eyes open no one home
trying to cram five hundred years
into a cardboard box
a flower maybe or a fern
holding hands all in a row and swaying side to side
in three-part harmony

stops that car sings
under way those waves of hope
into scatters dusk
still too close the smallest space she's dreamed
to text in

spirals coiled and big with child
I am many things says the old lady
but I am no chicken
I can run with the best of them

and beyond the rocks around her house
clearcut and alive still
forests wailing paining pink and yellowgreen
to muted browns greys beige
and all behind her
pulls her gaze to north
of whitetown
a great horned owl
perches
waiting
yak-iddy-yak-yak-yak

colder than crows on toboggans

the eggs were wrapped in doo doo
is what the auntys say
all those years
and hardly any rain
eggs all smooth and sweating
boiled hard around their yolks and greening words
staled by the years
the dozens and dozens of years
cocoon-like and floating
inside rain

the old lady stops that car says oh
we need our past   we need to remember
just look back   feel   smell   breathe   see them all
thank them for their medicines
thank them for their miracles
how to enjoy with the understanding of pain
the outpour of intimacy of love
safe and warm and free to breathe

and underneath the seat of that car little people dulled
and shy
belittled and afraid
alone
gone to church gone home
gone away
bye bye

this was early fall and very warm   the old lady's just a girl gets the
sickness in her chest   then she remembers that mother superior is
not a good word mother superior hurts baby

mother superior hates baby   baby's bad   bad baby bad girl   be
good always be good   like jesus they beat him and he cried but he
was still good   good is right and bad is wrong   love others   do
unto others as you would have them do unto you   hate yourself
    otherwise you are sinning against god

                                                            born to sin
                                                            squaw

that's when they all stop touching her
            they try to pull their feelings in
            cracked and rotting
            the old lady feels their fear
            how can anyone hate a baby is what goes through her head
            that's just before she sees them folks in whitetown
            put that baby in a vice
            and squeeze

some say she had problems with her mother   others say her mother
dies when she is young   dies of the smallpox or in her bed   they
bury her blanket with her just in case

at first she thinks it's that flubug
hurts all over
or maybe that white poison
that clings to her salt

all those years
motions mimes of empty words
in her bed in her bed
just sleep just sleep
make this pain go away
can't tuck her knees close enough
into her body

but she gets better
is what the auntys say
it's after that she walks
walks right out from the dusk
and glowing
even in the day

my people will sleep one hundred years
and when they awake
it will be the artists who give them back their spirit
a note the old lady finds frozen in hail the size of louis riel
ghost dancing with that giant butterfly

scared them folks in whitetown pretty good when they found her
in that vat
so many lifetimes eyes
wide open
sits right up says you folks are lucky
stomps right out of that vat like a giant
giant crow's what some of them say
others say a jackfish some a white pine
walks on that deadwater lake just to the left of whitetown
in a row ripple chat ripple
walks that water back to life that ripple sacred circle
water is life you sillys water is spirit food
your spirit's starving my relations
drink that water my relations
till you think you'll burst

and folks from whitetown crowd around
that old lady
big red hen by her side talking up a storm
your spirit's starving my relations
your sense of self is twisted
your past dead witches on the road
seen them from the window of my car
your sense of self is twisted

this keeps you from sensing your present sisters in the ditch
keeps you from grasping your future
women circles
four colours   black red yellow white   women circles keeping time

you hate you your own women how long did it take
to hate your own women eve mary sally jane
seven times a thousand years
your mirror mirror on the wall

smash that mirror with your fists
you stare at you yourself you hate you your own women
hate poison she

                                      womb spirit lingers

                and even if an egg could talk

33

                   you would hear a pin drop

and then you kill them cut them burn them up
in the cradle in the womb you hate you your own women
you learn to hate you as a child an infant as a babe
mommy doesn't like you right from the start
mommy doesn't
she says you try to feed him ribs
and apple pie
and then you put him out in the garden to die

that old lady heads out in her car big red hen warm wise
flies right up and over the landfill sight
lazy-legged lifts her butt that deadwater lake inside her eyes
tears the size of jackfish
and someone gets a picture
over by the landfill sight
the part where she looks down and turns around profound
how would you like my life for christmas or something

where there's a screech owl there's a passing
is what the auntys say
all muted browns greys beige
a round room
three doors one window
and out the mirror north

endless white noise wailing waiting
and in its wake

                              pages and pages of silence

why crow knows weendigo's not all he's cracked up to be

this is around the time them folks in whitetown invite the old lady to
speak about her mixed blood down at the united nations train station
museum   say to her you must have special objects moccasins
tomahawks scalps and skins being you're metis and she shows up
with her car big red hen warm wise which they get irate shake their
fists we want to know about your indian side   I am many things
says the old lady sucking on rat root   but I am no lollypop   I can
break wind with the best of them

that's right about the same time she starts to keep her writing
that same summer egg laying moon that old lady hides that
　　spoon
in that crows nest
and all them crows fight over that spoon for years
till that raven comes over from the landfill sight
eyes the size of jackfish
is what the auntys say

eleven days in court and even them crows can't cut a deal
that blackrobed judge with lemon in his eyes
big-mouthed and drooling
silver spoon potbellied right into his thighs
talking history whiteing out lies

says to them crows
make sure you ask for what it says here in the book
and there's only one answer and you can't look and hey
good luck
time's up
next

that's when them crows turn into hazelnuts
right there on the hardwood floor
and raven grabs that silver spoon
blackrobed judge and all
good thing the old lady gets it all down
before she heads out in her car
word for word she knows that short hand in her head
drives right up and over that landfill sight
out the window and lost in the view

every spring them crows show up right downtown whitetown year
by year and more on more on account of the kids and grandkids   got
lots of heart them crows   love to gossip love them rhymes   folks
in whitetown can't tell them crows apart can't understand crow
talk either   it's about late afternoon and picking up the sun and
them crows all singing hollow doo doo I'm a pip hollow doo doo pip
again   hollow doo doo give us a bingo to revive us again

that's just before them crows all up and light right there in downtown
whitetown all over the bar-strip drive   block off rush hour traffic
four hours straight   folks everywhere with cameras and
camquarters loonys and french fries   selling plastic crows on a
stick   each with a genuine hen feather   in drives that old lady
picks up all them crows takes them down to the bingo hall like they
ask   turns around yells out french fries french fries french fries for
sale   I am many things says the old lady but I am no driftwood   I
can hobdaub with the best of them

       it is said that upon the birth of a white buffalo
       the nations of the four directions black red yellow white
       will come together in unity
       a note the old lady finds frozen in hail the size of a miracle

wins the satellite then plays hide-and-seek with those crows
keeps them on their toes those crows
gets caught inside a three-trunked tree

at first she walks around with all that
wears those branches wears those leaves all over her face
there for the view

gives good shade is what the auntys say
a frogging we will go
a frogging we will go

hi ho the dairy-oh
a frogging we will go
is all she's able to say for four years straight
them folks down by the united nations train station museum
get a bit jumpy
specially at night

that's when the folks in whitetown bring in them tree doctors
three of them   one for each trunk
open your bark to our doctor eye
says those tree doctors
do you want us to push or do you want us to wait
by this time those tree doctors got safety glasses and chainsaws
hatchets and axes and steel toed boots
poised and ready for the kill

which is when the auntys get involved
show up at the train station united nations museum with little white
     dolls
the size of mosquitoes but only bigger
pinned to their coats their boots their hats their socks

proud women those auntys
teeny tiny tears pop out all around them
which they punctuate with an exclamation mark
splashes of white all in their path
on account of the dolls are wetsy betsy ever-tears

swirling curling churning around and around
a foreign language
out of the mouth and with the ears
their hollow bones they fill themselves with laughter

pretty soon those chainsaws fill up with water
a little on the salty side
pretty soon the united nations building fills up with water too
on account of the rapporteurs are in a meeting

pretty soon pretty much everything in whitetown
that's not tied down's bobbing drifting floating
foaming that dead water lake of whitetown
in a row ripple chat ripple chat
rat-a-tat-tat-tat

                    where there's a bullsnake there's a rattler
                    is what the auntys say
                    keeps her hand there steady calm sweat

halfrock halfleaf woman
voice like summer
and all that just before those folks in whitetown
finally let that old lady out of that three-trunked tree
fifty years they keep her in that three-trunked tree
for her own good for her writing her writing needs shape
feed her milk from cows and wheaties pork and beans
include all of you the white in you too
shakes her head yes no
words
dialogues of doo doo

shows up for supper with the auntys
double-breasted vest ribboned in the pines
bottom left button in the shape of a frog
biggest appetite you could imagine
eats a whole side of caribou and half a hind end too
eats for three days straight
then calls for all the kids to come around
is what the auntys say
tells them inside that three-trunked tree she met a
    wall
a wall who's everywhere yet can't be seen at all
whose bricks not red no smells of mother
no odors no taste no tone
yet this wall slimes her rots her in her sleep
starts to pick away at parts of her
shoves them in a bucket pulls them through a gate
so she builds objects hammers bats clubs batons
to replace her missing parts
then scrolls
out a window into sleep

full spring
the hills gone mad with rage
and that baby buffalo   birthed white
walks right out from that blizzard   downtown
whitetown crowds around   then
just as suddenly   in comes that giant
butterfly
one of them dark brown butterflies with the yellow-winged tips
bright like the sun   hovers
close to the round brown ground   voice
like blueing   shouts hey you
folks in whitetown listen up
in the name of god in the name of satan brothers arm in arms
didn't create you to injure all creation
all creation can't be you   you wear
your white skin eyes whose echo
flat and colourless   words of love
flow out of the mouth even while the hands are killing

and someone in whitetown gets a picture of that giant butterfly
inked like bleeding and reading against a blooming moon

42

and so the old lady gathers all the youth the kids the babes in
whitetown
moon all over her hair her teeth her arms
wide open
your spirit's starving my non-native relations
this keeps you hooked to your past dead indians on the plains
seen too many of them westerns on tv
your sense of self twisted
from knowing your present indians down the street
keeps you from the future healing circles
four colours black red yellow white circles keeping time

the old lady the youth kids babes black red yellow white
build around teeny tiny holes for wind and song
a giant bedsheet smooth and clean as flame

hang that sheet on a giant clothes line
hooked up between the tallest highrises in whitetown
one oil one bank
sixteen blocks apart

and there on that bedsheet giant eggs
red earth red and in the round
some say indian paintbrush some say poppy
some a red red rose

them giant eggs
birth butterflies in the millions all air and yellow air and yellow
bright like the sun
birth spiders too all black and water slick
articulate and kind
like grandmother moon

that's when that hatching moon comes right down into whitetown
sounds of flute so loud so long
next thing all them folks in whitetown
try to put that into words flat-lined across the page
not unlike loon songs
spirals horizons
music ancient of days
lingers   fingers on the page
fireflies in the millions

part ii
sharpening the hoofs on them horses

straddling them barebacked eggs

they say she flew right up into the sky
in the middle of the day
a speck and then a smudge
then shows up for supper with the auntys
biggest appetite you could imagine
eats a whole pot of meatball soup
and half a bannock too

then calls for all the kids to come around
tells them on her way to school she met an act
large and wild and not alive
yet that act has a body
sinks teeth deep into throats
and pulls away the flesh

the head is hollow
where a cord is there
down to the belly
that cord pulls endless in her hands
the present future in the past
little white creatures eating at that cord
growing in her throat an open hole
for wind to whistle pierces pine

a fear of winter where that act
finds a hole in the ice
a hole so deep the eyes can't see
that act's there still and waiting for the thaw

a nightmare
where sky
wears her through the day
corroded pewter
browned to gentle dusk

where time

keened and slowed to green
sways her gaze skyward
there geese
in the millions vee'd
luminesced and rageful loud

combust

goes to school with all that in her hair her skin her eyes
open and opening to
wide she can see now
first day and many lifetimes
same school same street
four hundred years and not a day without the pain
yearstearsfears

listen

the governor in council may by order declare that the indian breed
and his breed wife and minor unmarried children are enfranchised
a note the old lady finds frozen in hail the size of a horseshoe

at school they told her she was mad
is what the auntys say
it's true she was tired
so tired she starts with writing in her sleep
over to the left and all in rows
of smiling faces
teachers drill and stuffing in their eyes
they all hold sticks or pointers magic wands
high above their heads
and speak together one by one in unison
of pains inside their paunches
crooked lies

best grade nine she ever had that old lady
comes right on in there and yells out
french fries
french fries
french fries for sale
and all those smiling faces line up in a row
and out they walk into the cold

and in walks the old lady
picks up all them magic wands
packs them over at the united nations train station museum
where she turns princes into frogs
and then she has a feast of feasts
near the beginning of the frosts
corn squash and pole beans
frybread frogslegs eggs and greens
dripping grease and keeping time

they say that was the coldest winter they could remember
minus forty-two and holding sundogs
days and running days
deer and elk moose and magpie horse and raven
all move right downtown whitetown for a spell
pick up some of them magic wands and mirrored shades from the
      old lady
keep them suns out of their eyes
while they try their luck at changing princes into frogs
pretty soon there's folks with their cameras inside their cars all over
      the place
snap snap says those cameras
snap snap snap

folks get so used to them double suns sunny side up   over at the
school till them sundogs start to come in threes their song a piercing
haunting wailing sound   where beauty meets with pure and lethal
hate   spiritselves and pineing

                         just to be

      at school they told her she was a no-good slut
      said she'd have a baby like all the rest of them squaw-girls
      a system made to measure for the gang
      prettify the language faking calm for flat bare hate
      content to cruel and back again
      that's the year it snowed right through the spring and into june
      that old lady only twelve years old
      ashamed of her fear
      shaking fetal lost in the view

                                                        51

      starting at the back the way she looks at magazines
      breaking through the pain
      reads between the stories sees the lies
      that's when she fills out one of them ads for horse manure
           delivery
      bills it to the school
      flew that manure all the way from texas

is what the auntys say
dumped it right there in front of the school
principal couldn't do a darn thing on account of the snow
blocked the view from the windows poop and snow poop and snow
sure smelled around that school
and all the way over at them badlands and deep deep in the pines

that's when all them crows drop in for a while

    poop all over the windows of the school

poop all over that horse poop too   make so much noise caw cawing
fart farting laugh laughing sing singing dance dancing caw cawing

                    in comes the whitetown
swat team slipping on that poop all in their pistols all in their hair

                    out of the blue

in crawls all the babys in whitetown   brown themselves up pretty
good   take them pistols right out from under the swat teams noses
and throw them

up

        up

   up

and to the crows all in rhythm all in rhyme singing cawing dancing
out from

                                                        time

and out pops that big red hen poop scratches on the road

in hops all the babys tie scarfs around their heads   fill up that
big red hen warm

   wise

      open the moon roof all the windows on account of the smell

that big red hen creamy smooth soft kind stops for that old lady and

her just twelve years old

                    tears the size of jackfish

someone gets a picture all browns ember red and burning against a
blue sky moon

at school they told her she was simple
well thinks that old lady I certainly haven't been keeping time
reflection in words and so much going on
fear of their fear
this is the same afternoon they think she dances for the class
gets so hot all them gophers running about outside
thinking it's full spring
kids all in the windows yelling hey look at all them gophers
that old lady must be dancing up there in eleventh grade

understanding the dreams would help
and so she dances
right there on top of the teacher's desk
kids all in the windows see them crows
cold-dulled and scrawny
over on them telephone lines
up there for air or rapid water
firey cold and tossing a silver spoon
singing hold me hold me love me hush hold me hold me love me
sweet something

waiting for that moment for the my the me
thoughtmemorys in print and bouncing off them wires
all crowy wavy lines
right through them windows and in to that old lady

by this time everyone even all them teachers line up in the halls
even the principal that girl's in a league all her own
and so she dances hurt angry threatened on guard left out
poison verbal poison voice is sacred
spewing in invisible erased
case history case closed

they say she sang like grandmother moon
even in the day
could hear her way over at them badlands and deep deep
in the pines
is what the auntys say
that old lady loves them badlands
sticks them pine cones in her hair and sings up the dust
gets herself one of them fancy stereos over at the crowsnest
then heads east on a prairie highway on them hot hot summer days
clover smells to bursting buffy blaring in the breeze
sun fills that air lush growing green

that's when it happens
when she's close up to that crest
happens every time
when she's close up to that crest
chest fills to bursting
glee
glee she
so close up to that crest
every time that old lady's here it's still the same this land who
calls her by her name

a horse's nest egg is very large

at school they said her face must be erased from the crowd
this is grade four and just after she wins the national poetry contest
cameras camquarters and her just an earshot away
cold on the outside quiet warm calm inside
holding back the sadness
to herself

                                         eyes
                                         that teacher

you must not say these things
you must consider your audience
you must never under any circumstance
disempower the powerful
please censor your story
and remember we are having this conversation in strictest
confidence
the smell of hair spray at the nose

        that's when her mouth goes all thin and tinny
        sour air and shame inside her whole
        heart mommys daddys grannys grampas
        auntys uncles cousins thighs hips arms
        maintains remains her silence anger grows
        over and over

her heart bursts out to river
smooths a clearing on the page

the written word does not have to be wrapped in the thoughts of the
colonizer
a note the old lady finds frozen in hail the size of connie fife
sweat hoboing with that giant butterfly

and there's that teacher from her school
who speaks from over to the left and all in rows
on that new tv all black and white and smiles and white white teeth
embrace and welcome to whitetown
yes she's brilliant for a young sauvage
her favourite food is french fries and there's something about her
writing
lazy and arrogant
like a rich french dessert

the auntys watch that on tv
laugh and laugh and eat popcorn with extra butter
clinging to their salt
them folks can't read worth beans
is what the auntys say
they got it right there on the kitchen wall
all framed with the old lady smiling tight
her false teeth right there beside her in a cup
she makes that cup at the senior high
paints words on it too
uses the extra paint left over from her car
big red hen red

words are jewels is what she writes on that cup

words are jewels

grains of rice to kneel on depending on the view

they say that fear runs deep
says the old lady
how deep says the auntys
deep deep says the old lady
so says the auntys
just so we know

wind and water and very few people
recurring dream in a dentist chair
and there she is that old lady
sitting in front of her computer
putting the finishing touches off the line
and there they are
the grandmothers
all talking all at once

well blow me over with a feather
says that big red hen warm wise
woman of few words that one
loves to eat with the grandmothers
just like that horse says those auntys
comes for dinner and then moves out of reach
cracks a good joke every time though

doesn't have to look for an audience
words herself around pretty good
non-verbal too

                              those teachers down in whitetown

what is essay poem story   any deviation is a

                                        sin

                         can't see can't read
                         outside their writing on the wall
                         floors doors windows
                         all squared and mirrored in

which is what that old lady learns at school
learns how to swear learns how to lie
around the same time that halfbreed girl from whitetown says
I'm a two-spirit I thought you were a two-spirit too
and that old lady says no
these are just my eyes   held
the other day though
such power of body   lifted
breath gone heart   oh
such wonder   my my my
says the old lady
                         I'm in love

my my my

          says

               that big red hen warm wise

it's a miracle
but first let me get this kraft dinner out from
underneath my false teeth
the ones on the bottom are all mine got none at the back but
the front ones they look fine

       one minute I'm burping over there at the library
       downtown whitetown and some guy says pick it up

my my my

        so good so close

close so close   touching
warm soft smells so good
nuzzle necks shoulders   melting
aroused and lifted   my my my

oh my and there's that giant butterfly
laughs talking through the moon
her yellow shining very yellow for the sun
and all the men in whitetown little boys
playing hockey on the road
a very wonderful evening
safe quiet sexy happy day
the sameness of being with a woman

supportive though surprised is what the auntys say
getting the words out one by one
you flow like water waves onto the air
my my my says the old lady I am many things
but I am no horsefly
I can score with the best of them

                        going home

        where even the smallest egg

smells loving red between the leaves

                   powerful and soft

       click click click
       says that old lady's tongue
       click click click

we tell our girl cook a little for a feast
go to sweat lodge purify yourself
rebirth your body
mind heart spirit
then go on with our story even though the pain

we tell her prepare share this recipe les boulettes
for those who love ground meat
two pounds lean ground meat
medium onion chopped nice and fine
pinch of salt and we like lots of pepper
one half cup of flour mixed into the meat to hold and mix well
then roll into two or three inch balls and roll in flour again then
place in about four cups of boiling lightly salted water and
simmer gently for an hour

smells good hey
takes your mind to a good place when you cook my girl
put all your love
into what you prepare
thank the plants the animals who give up their lives
remember your ancestors who gave up theirs
put out a plate for them
feed them

we tell her one day when quebec wakes up
there'll be seven million more metis
many metis grandmothers didn't know their metis grandmothers
for generations already and still today you'll hear their
daughters
say I am proud to be metis
a beautiful long and roaming song a slogan
joining of two cultures a distinct nation of people
forever

generation after generation story after story
in the public and separate schools
and you tell us the same stories your daughters tell too
some still in foster care
town after town

little girls having the wisdom of an old woman just to stay alive

all the stories sound the same now but back then
there was nowhere to go for help
not that there's so much help out there today our kids still
pushed past childhoods
same old lines
lies on the walls in the halls
in the little children's history books
about savages and tipis scalps and great spiritual leaders
of the olden times
like we and our languages all died off
with the royal proclamation
and now it's still just a matter of time

that meatball soup and just about anything
tastes great with bannock my girl
four cups flour
one half cup melted shortening
four teaspoons baking powder
pinch of salt
one and a half cups cool water
mix the dry well and mix the water and shortening then mix
everything together until you are able to knead about five times
then press into a nice circle nine ten inches around and bake at
three hundred seventy-five degrees for about half hour

the mouth of an egg is a horse's arse

pressure of unwashed tears   of water salted
self-contained   level-headed
seen it all   egg wash for scone
old macdonald had a farm   a nest egg
protected by the shell   depend on farms
incomes slaughter   in the light
scripted golden   eee-eye-eee-eye-oh

potato eggs raw or lightly steamed grate into patties they'll hold
things together well enough

white pine in her body smiles the breeze
firey and bright and clear
a beautiful and powerful woman
a life within a life
she is a canadian citizen and her problems are therefore

small

story within a story framing happy glory day
as long as the rivers flow is what the auntys say
her country takes her needs
her country takes her children
her children's children's children

a truant officer may take into custody any indian breed child
whom he believes on reasonable grounds
to be absent from school
using as much force as the circumstances require
a note the old lady finds frozen in hail the size of an egg beater

most health food stores carry
egg replacer

at school they told her she was a wagon burner
that's where she learns to work like a horse
fists boots and bile
glass beads and metal crosses
like dew worms on the snow
stiff and black

which is just before her first foster home in whitetown which is just
before the foster farm which is just before the sixth foster home in
whitetown which is just before the war in europe

which is just before the folks in whitetown
invite the old lady to speak about her metis ancestors
down at the writers retreat
which she tells them she's seen family friends elders babes
murdered and mutilated
seen ravenblack brown braids hanging from a white picket fence
different sizes textures styles

and no one speaks to her after that   three days of silence
and then vegetarian breakfast in bed

served by one of her teachers from the senior high the one
who shows the old lady how to make a mug

whispers it's so wonderful that you have so much love to
give

after all you've been through
no eye contact   lifts her eyes looks   looks down at the old lady
whispers break them in slowly you have to break them in

gently

flax eggs three tablespoons equals one egg a healthy alternative to
high cholesterol eggs great for pancakes breads and other baking

lost under heavy pain
is what the auntys say

so much pain and still that old lady

pulling out pleasure from under every crack in the sand

happy and beautiful with braided hair
taking all that dreamtime and giving so much back
lights a fire at first light
lights a fire and thanks our creator
for this new day
this new life

the eggs were stuffed with horsehair

at school they told her she was a woodenhead
looks up that one in the dictionary
and there it is
just before wooden indian just after wood engraving
a game of chess on the hardwood floor

in the trunk of that giant car them eggs
grainfed and newsprint on their yolks
their crowns their rumps
wombed and woven in

and there's the old lady
green with specks of silver in her hair
gardening over by the landfill sight
filling in those spaces with her breath
a voice so soft and comfort in a storm

those walking mouths
whose bodies
couldn't love
those talking bodies
whose mouths
wouldn't love

and seeing in her shining
bright wings
that
salty taste
of everything

apple sauce eggs three tablespoons great for sweeter recipes

like the day all those whitetown kids were playing ga-lahs
over by the landfill sight
forest all around
and down swoops that young eagle
spotted eagle all puffed and beautiful
takes those kids a while to stop that game to look
where eagle plays

and there not far away
light like sun comes up and through the ground
wide and round
a lake and not a lake
bees hover near the top

and out climbs all those little people
roots and barks drums and shopping carts
climb up on eagle's back
sing

hey you kids from whitetown while you may
wear that cedar in your sneakers every day
only simple goodness will come your way
walk that goodness in your heart and in your play
and you need never fear come night or day

and all those little people drum drumming sing singing dance dancing
braiding the manes of horses all round and fine
knotting up all them clothes on the clotheslines
hanging moccasins and little gifts for kids for babes
way up high in them white pines

                                    my mother is woman is me

72

                        my past is dead is me

a note the old lady finds frozen in hail the size of pumpkins

this is around the endtime of the witch hunts
that story long and many deaths along the way
white women in the millions
their fathers brothers uncles grampas too
whose shadows in their wake
a game of jacks behind the bar
track them little people

        them little people
        dulled and shy
        belittled and afraid
        alone
        gone to church gone home
        gone away
        bye bye

there's where they hide shaking fetal lost
under the seat of that car big red hen warm wise
their sleeps won't have to dream

banana eggs are great for desserts or sweets or smoothies one half
banana mashed

at school they told her she was shooting herself in the foot
had a good aim that old lady specially as a girl
that was just before the telephones
the tree poles
heavy and dark against a clear blue sky
she's up there near the top of one of them poles
and running on the wires
uses one of them magic wands from the school to keep her straight
in time

       that was after she writes her lines
       I will not shoot myself in the foot
       I will not shoot myself in the foot
       I will not shoot myself in the foot
       I will not shoot myself in the foot
       seven thousand hundred times
       runs so fast along them wires she converts

   to light

         they hear to think she's lightening
         water's what some of them say
         rapid water
         firey cold and voicing
         on the page

now how am I going to put the mother back in the language
because in my language
and in my culture
as well as indian people's cultures
mother is the land
a note the old lady finds frozen in hail the size of maria campbell
storytelling with that giant butterfly

all those eggs and just one basket
the good red reads along the river road
which is about the same time that raven swoops right down
and grabs that clock right out from the bottom of that river
swallows it whole

throws off her rhythm for the longest time
can't find her mother
that's when she remembers
when a babe doesn't feel the bigness of her mother's love
the girl feels the bigness of that love from river
mother river
mother river's passions deep and into the pores of the spirit

that's where the old lady drops off all them little people
says hi all you little people
this is where you get off
come with me and close your eyes
close your eyes and imagine you're sitting
on the bottom of the river

and there they are
look up and see sun the moon all rapid water firey cold
caress of river cool all warm

those little people tell her oh
we know now
we know
terror we couldn't acknowledge because of the doubt
doubt we couldn't understand because of the terror
and they those little people
cradled in the arms of the grandfathers
so's not to be pulled away
there's where they stay

a soft south wind

coaxes   sand

where utter   pain

silent and

little spirit moon

between the cracks

tofu eggs soft tofu well mixed one half cup

        that rock they tied to her leg
        wouldn't float
        is what the auntys say
        this is not too long after the old lady drops off those little people
        same river same cradle
        says hi on her way down
        asks them do they have anything to eat
        she's real hungry
        nearly starve her to death before they tie that rock to her leg
        if the truth be known

     those little people tell her oh
     we know now
     we know
     we internalize the selfhate here
     right here and here and here
     in our bodys

     until we bring these two together
     our bodys are our spirit homes
     until we bring these two together
     in time
     we hate

well that's sure good to know
says the old lady
rock untied and floating to the top
good thing you know that short hand in your head

they say she let her body mind go to sleep

                              and with her spirit mind

        moves out of her body

                    into the too zone is what the auntys say

        where

    touch

                        she reaches out her feelings

78

                            rounds colours water
                            rich and soft
                            fine-line yellowed
                            blues to purpled green
                            deep and slow
                            deliberate

part iii
you must break them apart until the children are read

soft melodies of tumbleweed on smooth brown eggs

they say trauma heightens the awareness
wish it was that simple says the old lady to those little people
past future present to be reckoned with
tears like torrent corndoll ragdoll inside out
like off the frames of a reel of film
cropped and powerful

sure got lively down there in that river
well at least we heard the right words says those little people
breathing the breeze a thin line crack a light
up and down their bodies
tickles the hairs above the lip the neck the legs
laughter from the kitchen smells of frybread smells of grease

late late nights of love bodys close touching peace happy
asleep and drifting laughter from the kitchen
dreams of bear and water
follow that bear little people follow that bear
bear knows where the water is shame shadows cradles
seeps the past

and through to present those little people all dressed up
shoreline rushing by bright daylight warm of air
the cool of river on their bottoms through the leaves
and floating in the hundreds for the feast

twirling a lock of her hair

around and around

a foreign language

like english

where seven out of ten words are french
the english fight the french
the french fight the english
the french and english and others
try to extinguish all others
whenever they have the chance

a story the old lady writes in school

reads out that story later on the upright radio tick-talk show
reads straight out at the audiences in their kitchens
looks out over them wires just before the noxema ad and just after
    tide
this is around postwar crackdown on the indian problem in canada
I am many things says the old lady drawing out her love
but I am no double-barreled shotgun
I can egg in the face with the best of them

but the stable eggs have ears

them indian problem officers them robed ones
they take away her babys three four hundred years
right out from around their mommys daddys grannys grampas auntys
uncles cousins
thighs hips arms
her babys she'd loved them held them rocked them sang to them
seven thousand hundred times

any indian problem officer may deem to be a juvenile delinquent and
take into custody
any indian breed child
using as much force as circumstance requires
a note the old lady finds frozen in hail the size of a well beaten egg

her first two babys die on account of the flubug tb measles
    smallpox
common cold
is what the auntys say
takes years to recover from the grief
the mystery of death won't bear those little buds to bloom

and now these blackrobed bandits
crowd right into whitetown a paper big as your arm
bless this paper bless this home
what's here on this paper is superior is right
that paper declares death in life for her babys
heard that older squaw-girl was trying to take over the
    school

it's after that she withdraws

deep deep

deep deep

calm to her bones

it's after that she takes to writing
writing out the silence writing out the pain
there's where there's a teacher from her school
who speaks from over to the left and all in rows and says
she knows people as well as the great writers and she is
very
talented
it's the white in her makes her write that way

the auntys laugh and laugh and eat egg rolls with extra chicken
clinging to their salt
them folks can't read worth beans
is what the auntys say
they got it right there on the hallway wall
all framed and with the old lady smiling bright her false teeth
right beside her is a cup
she makes that cup at the senior high
paints words on it too
uses the extra paint left over from her car
big red hen red
creator I'm reaching out to you
take me home creator
take me home

that round brown face
under a fresh foundation
put there by her foster mothers hand the hand that beats her
                              yes we've been abused
says her foster mothers
the hand that ties those dead chickens around her neck
leaves them there for days

                    as women we experience sexism
        the hand that feeds her slop with bluegreen spots
        just before the hogs get the rest

                    as we get older we encounter ageism
        the hand that controls electric fences keeps her in the yard
        white picket fences face the road
        dupes the neighbours dupes them all

                yes
says her foster mothers
                yes
                we develop feelings for all the little heathens we
                raise up
                for extended periods of time
rifle cocked and aims right for her godless little heart
that's just before she chases the little slut out the front door
and down to the welfare office

we all have to be careful with our time around here
says that woman at the welfare office
we all have to make room for the other poor children
children much worse off than you my dear
now go on back there and behave yourself or
we'll have to put you
in the zoo with the other animals

*we tell our girl take another break go make some supper for the
    kids*
while we decide how to deal with the teach rhymes with preach
keeping the non-natives ignorant is the main goal in the schools
in the universities
*our kids our youth always looking between the lines for their
    truth*
generation after generation

duncan campbell scott indian agent travelling treaty man gone
poet who believed with all his heart in the power of his savage
lines their power to tame to blame to genocide the wild creatures
of the woods and canoes
such silly talk and still today

ignorance means so much we tell her
when there's land all over the country that belongs to our great
    nations
titled crown land to confuse the many who still think we're dying

or lying from our fourth world view
it's time to negotiate unceded land
it's time to admit crown land is land that belongs to the first
    peoples
disturbed agreements made

in hopes we and our languages would all die off or we'd kill
one another
or starve to death fighting ever-enforced poverty or the indian
act abolished or
the white paper or the treaties rendered null and void
in hopes the royal proclamation mute
before the leases expire

the wild creatures speak the english and french pretty good now
and are ready to
take back the land our mother with grace and love
the leases are up and

oops we're still here

banging our heads against thick brass doors where one-sided
    law
changes on a dime
year after year after decades after all

what reasons could there be
why do non-natives in canada think the hooks of the
government puncture our bodies
so deeply for effect the fear factor
savage lines in their news to keep their myth alive with
imaginations run wild
the goal still the same to obliterate the core of our children's
    spirits

they may be thinking we aren't nations like theirs always have
been ancient knowledge reaching out to our youth
what are they thinking those non-native people
who just want us to get over it all without serving up the table
    first
and move on

that's when that old lady remembers coils torso arms her hands
touches echo hollow sorrow
howls the day

hears the wind in the air the water odors warm of sun
the cool of the trees

the real of the round brown ground
the bugs the birds the animals

remembers feels the love their faces
the gifts from the grandmothers and grandfathers

her mommys daddys grannys grampas auntys uncles cousins
thighs hips arms

their faces
their faces who heal
their faces
who give her life
right at the level of life

that's when those words to speak they disappear

                                    and make like song

            that old lady is song

    that old lady is song

                        sings glee sings glee to lift to see

        oh lucky me

rinsing off the whites of eggs

something like the morning she wakes up in the middle of a
dream
takes that   dream   to breakfast and before she knows any
better
eats part of that   dream   for breakfast too
that's when she notices

        that's when she feels like red orange leaf
        bright against a bluebacked sky
        floating glowing fills the breeze
        she's mother mentor sister peace calm companion
        lovehold passions healing love
        coaxes dances singing sings
        words out to voicing for the sky

        that same day the old lady stops by for the feast and giveaway
        back packed big as a house
        cans of cedar jars of sage
        and dozens and dozens of jackfish
        all cleaned and wrapped and brave
        that's the time the old lady can't stop eating
        biggest appetite you could imagine
        eats a whole pot of moose stew
        and half a jackfish too

then calls for all the kids to come around
tells them how that morning
sky all ochre red
whiskey jacks and crows
and out swims all them jackfish
right out from under them reeds rhymes with reads
as if with lungs and wings and old and bold
they swim the air a circle

placing rocks around her house
their talk of laws and jaws
of teeth on the palate teeth on the tongue
nasty bite them jackfish
don't like to break water
is what the auntys say
strength of a thousand fish
when they're hooked

and there from the middle of that lake
a fear of winter where that act
whose hole in the ice
a hole so deep the eyes can't see
and out climbs all them blackrobed folks from whitetown
potbellys brained by booze and frostbite on their knees
their fingers frozen to the line
that act's there too all smiles and hi smiles and hi
hands high in the name of the father the son in the name of
the holy ghost
marching singing one by one in unison
amazing grace how sweet the sound
was blind but now I see

tired of the fight the fuss the fury
and oh how she loves to   teach
is what the auntys say
sings that bundle of reeds rhymes with   reads
right over her shoulder and onto her back

and right away the mayor of whitetown wants to know
sends the native liaison worker to find out what's in the pack

the native liaison worker makes tea and cornbread

bannock hamburger soup berry soup rice pudding scone with raisons
elk stew boiled moose meat baked in rich thick gravy raw kidney
blueberry pie

frybread greens indian tacos fresh fruit salad chokecherry jam
buffalo burgers
for the old lady

who reads to that native liaison worker   day after day

looks up says it is very bad form to seek to speak to a person
when they are busy

wind blowing earthy tunes day and night day and night
same colours as the northern lights   same looks   same
power too

crow doesn't tell bear's story
a note the old lady finds frozen in hail the size of a goose egg

which is just before them crows settle in them houses
on account of the friendly fire deep deep in the sacred pines
ravens too depending on the view
poop all over that razor wire
poop all over them peace missiles
block up the holes in them security tanks
and they all sit down one day
and make a drawing of their love

aboriginal reality
in canada has beco
me a vicious circ
le of cause and effec
t if that vicious circle is to beco
me a healing circle
the roots of injustice must be addressed
instead of problem feeding problem
solution must feed solution
a note the old lady finds frozen inside hail the size of georges
erasmus
fasting with that giant butterfly

offers arms voice soothes gentle of touch hold on hold
cut the pain in half to taste its nectar candied sweet
eyes closed feel the feel
half-night half-day moment

poached eggs deviled blue-eyed blind

which is right after she escapes from that psychosurgery ward
gut sick sinking hearing seeing somewhere in the air
skinned eyes whose echo
detached and observing
open your wounds to our doctor eye
we see she's made up of leafy stuff and rock the colour of blood

only after they discover she has a crack in her skull
seven fingers wide and she insists
she's had that crack four hundred sixty-seven years

all this time she's been unable to open up
is what the auntys say
unable to find the words to put that crack
where her mouth ought to be
stays the silence mists of shame

reaches knows hears all those little people
untie that grandfather rock from around her leg
and bring her breakfast in bed

and now today the mother gives back

                out and to the sun
                        all rare and wondrous
                                wet and sweet

even down there in whitetown

a dream without a view

        houses hunched together
        frightened chickens side by each and two by two

        all those picket fences lined up in a row hup-two-three-four
        hup-two-three-four and feeling like part of the group

        where's the love and who knows who
        mean and lazy

96
                a foreign language
                like english

                heavy with nouns and frowns
                and flat like fly paper to the ear

                a swarm of june bugs aphids ants

out of the mouth and scribbled on the wall in one hour blurbs
so much waste in their wake
and winter still lingers in the sand
in the belly of the badlands

                              writes like she eats
                              slowly until each mark
                              each swallow
                              is new

         new like a red red prairie sky
         thirty below and clouds morning rolling breathing
         thunder on a hot hot summer day
         is what the auntys say

part iiii
many mothertongued and too big for that one

full-winged and awed to cheechauk

water on the window
five hundred years and all those white sheep
in the wake of the view
paleskinned blueyed baby
not my cup of tea
says her mommy that hot brown day

everyone even the sky could see
the round of mother earth
the prairie
the mountains
inside that baby's eyes
displaced misplaced
out of place

one side of her body
the left side
smooth moonlight
hatred on both sides
fearful glances from the pines

101

and out pops the old lady
body raining flying fills the breeze
picks up that paleskinned blueyed baby
how can anyone hate a baby is what goes through her head
this is just after she sees them folks in whitetown
put that baby in a vice
and squeeze

we believe the relationship between aboriginal
and non-aboriginal people
in canada
must change
we believe it can
the cycle of blame and guilt
grievance and denial
frustration and fear
can be broken
it is time to renew
to turn the page
a note the old lady finds frozen in hail the size of rene dussault
feasting on tick-talk radio with that giant butterfly

calls out all the relations
from behind the pines behind the picket fences
we're here to feel says the old lady to the folks that day
to feel in our spirits with out hearts bodys minds
to feel the beauties of this place
this place where time is held
and space is stilled

holds that baby to her heart
this babe is sacred all my relations
your hooks of hate
fearful pierce
see here
and here and here
and here
hands that paleskinned blueyed baby
to her blackeyed brownskinned mommy

lifts her fingers to her throat an open hole
for wind to whistle pierces pine
a hook is there is partly loosed
and growing out
a leafy red a day or two away

                       and on that hook a fishing line
                       finds a hole in the ice
                       a hole so deep the eye can't see
                       inside and down and down

there are those who think they pay me a compliment in saying
that I am just like a white woman
my aim my joy my pride
is to sing the glories of my own people
ours is the race that taught the world that avarice veiled by any
      name
is crime
a note the old lady finds frozen in hail the size of pauline johnson
gifting with that giant butterfly

that night she has a dream

          so brief so vivid

                       she's high above the ground

perhaps the rockys appalachians laurentides

vision carved to clear

barehilled plains whose rivers   oil-slicked and mirrored inward

bleed the land

the land

clearcut and unpeopled

to the east   above the belly of the round   dulled silver leaks the
    sky

bare-armed and starve the beast

there's a fiction between us and them
is what the auntys say
at their schools they call it history
headlines in their news

what they call
all those mountain hiking boots lined up in a row hup-two-three-four
hup-two-three-four and feeling like part of the group
sing long and loud in three-part harmony
a logging we will go
high-ho the dairy-oh
a logging we will go

what they call reforestation adopt a pine
signs along the roads
crews of planters pioneers
macho whitetown's last frontier
payment by the tree
keeps the kid in university

holy crow and sweat upon the brow
of empty eyes and designer shorts
which makes it worth the work

there's ebb and then there's flow
singing long and singing glee
there were trees
trees
as big and knobby knees
in the store
in the store
there were trees
trees
as big as knobby knees
in the corner master store

plant a moose plant a bear
adopt a salmon or a hare
a note the mayor of whitetown finds frozen in hail the size of a
maple leaf

rich and gentle love the great tree people they are creator's breath

their wisdoms   heal us   seven times a thousand years   their

forest-breath and broadest shoulders in the world   wear them in our

bones   is what the auntys say   billions of great tree people

whose trail of tender tears   or trophies   depending on the view

past present future to be reckoned with

wind grass and water birds
words refracted
readjust the text
read just what's on the page
lips inked in and darkness all around

the metisse weave

pecking round a plate of eggs after a rain
and then the dog who is the sky
blue with fluffy clouds in the shapes of animals and trees
pops out from hail the size of a jack-in-the-box
froze right in there a piece of paper wound around his neck
rare and wonder
and on that paper it is said when taking something from the earth
always explain to the spirit of the animal or plant why
and in return for the generosity and help shared so freely
offer some tobacco in a nice clean place

    sometimes things are just so simple
    is what the auntys say
    early morning both doors open air and sun and wondered
    like joy and love life and laughs
    a smile a breeze all envied green
    for a life that plays mellow music
    through giant speakers in the sky

like the time they put the photo of that giant butterfly
one of them dark brown butterflies with the yellow-winged tips
bright like the sun
inked like blueing and reading against a berry moon sky
put that photo up on a billboard over at the football stadium
hockey rinks golf clubs race tracks malls theatres
united nations train station museum

put a slogan on that poster
how much bud could a bud man chug
if a bud man could chug bud

which is the same weekend the paparazzi convention
golfing down by the united nations train station museum
point their cameras camquarters skyward black and blue all over
crows ravens magpies in the millions
flying being pulling at the horizon
trigger them streetlights neon signs
adults screaming j-running blocking up traffic all over the place

and all the kids in whitetown
toddlers pets flashlights strollers wheelchairs blankets guitars
grab their three-d glasses red and blue
and head for the billboards
red squiggly lines move up from the round brown ground
all around and on those billboards

become a giant egg
one of them freerange grainfed eggs
brown with dinosaurs and fish birds and frogs snakes and bugs
hidden inside in all manner of movement and time

whose slogan
fluorescents edged in black
rougarou and how do you do
it is better to have a hen tomorrow
than an egg today

and all the parkades in whitetown
the lots the metres the stalls the booths
up and fly the coop
my my my says that big red hen warm wise
my my my

we tell our girl wherever you go whatever you do always
*   remember*
the three sisters who would never be apart from one another

sisters to be planted together eaten and celebrated together
pole beans and corn and squash
companions who run deep into our bodies keep our spirits
*   strong*

take the time to bake to savour   cheddar corn muffins
one cup cornmeal   one cup all-purpose flour
one teaspoon sugar   one teaspoon salt
one teaspoon baking soda   one and one half teaspoons
one and one half cups   baking powder
buttermilk   two eggs
one cup thawed frozen corn   one cup sharp shredded
*   cheddar*
one quarter cup melted butter or margarine
preheat oven to four hundred degrees and coat twelve muffin
cups with cooking spray
combine in a bowl cornmeal flour baking powder sugar salt
and soda and set aside
mix together buttermilk eggs and butter and stir into corneal
mixture with corn and cheese and bake about twenty-five
minutes

in the same way always remember the spirits of the great buffalo
before and after old macdonald made a new sport
standing in train cars and open slaughter
on those who stood helpless around the tracks
afraid to cross the metal lines
averaged five thousand dead buffalo a day for three years
    straight
these men and boys with guns whose
fathers uncles cousins grandfathers brothers who'd already
killed one way or another
thirty times as many first peoples by then

what do you suppose they were thinking my girl
what do you suppose they told their
children
not that we were one hundred and fifty million strong
but that we were a handful of savages running about
in all manner of bare nakedness
killing one another with tomahawks and spears
such silly talk and we know what they tell their children now

same old things
won't face the shame
not their shame they say not their blame not their responsibility
can't help what those old guys did way back when

they truly believe first peoples can go to university for free
get money all over the place
which of course isn't true but what can you say to people who
don't even know first peoples
were banned from university
until this generation
even if a person could that person would cease to be native
and to top it all couldn't be a professional a doctor lawyer

teacher pharmacist dentist university professor
no matter how many university degrees
until this generation

seven generations ago a home where the buffalo roamed
in numbers that would boggle
a home where the great white pine once housed the vast eastern
*   farmlands*

our grandmothers talked of white man loans
borrowed from the eastern farming nations trapping nations
to build universities and roads and railways
loans that were written off in the courts within the year and
it is said the equivalent of six billion never repaid
farms that were paid for fair and square by the eastern nations
were seized and the first peoples herded onto reserves and
oh my how the list goes on

in the same way always remember your sisters
your grandmothers who once were girls
the looks on their faces when they met those hens those wonderful
birds
who give freely their eggs themselves
to nourish our bodies
always honour their spirits and pray for them today
the way they're farmed all that fear in their meat in their eggs
you buy at the supemarkets
their spirits in need
their meaning not merely contained by the eggs themselves
and nothing more

and always remember to pray for the return of our mother the
*   land*

my my my

which is years before she meets them women from the rez
on the downtown whitetown bus
the ones who go to the university
who singsong hey whitetown halfbreeds
apples on a log
whitetown metis
wannabees in a fog

then them women from the rez
ink on their fingers ink on the floor
in the corners of their mouths
cracked and caked and frothing
take a picture of the old lady

over by the united nations train station museum

that's when the old lady hands them hammers bats clubs batons
tells them break down the mirrors break down the walls
that old lady heads out in her car
with them women from the rez

tie scarfs around their heads and fill up that big red hen warm wise
drive right up and over the landfill sight
lazy-legged lifting butts that dead water lake inside their eyes
tears the size of jackfish

when you lose something my girls
you gain tenfold
says the old lady as she takes them women from the rez
and shows them
the universe
I am many things says the old lady drinking chokecherry tea
but I am no snow white
I can moon on water with the best of them

it's just after that them folks from whitetown   dullwitted and middle
of the road   browse around and in the pines   just getting through
the file   is what them robed ones say   all smiles and hi smiles and
hi   what we learned in books is superior is right   there's policies
there's facts   says right here in black and whitepaper wide as a
mile   a note them robed ones find frozen in hail the size of a red ant
egg   and pretty soon   her mommys daddys grannys grampas
auntys uncles cousins   enfranchised disentailed   her life story
can't say she's indian   can't say she's not   a sign and nailed onto
the door   star light star bright   first star I see tonight   I wish I
may I wish I might   I'll huff and I'll puff and

she is reading her blanket with her hands

a note the old lady finds frozen in hail the size of lee maracle
drinking tea on the hardwood floor with that giant butterfly that eagle
that owl that big red hen warm wise them eggs them little people
them crows ravens magpies
I am not interested in gaining entry to the doors of the white
women's movement
I would look just a little ridiculous sitting in their living rooms saying
we this and we that

        that river those trees that sand those rocks
        the air the sun the sky
        they are who give the most along the way
        is what the auntys say
        feel the water
        under the skin
        the colour of heartroot
        across the page over and over
        and over and

slow enough to stay between the lines
moving on in life and expressing a love that won't find a place
in ordinary terms

like the year they managed to blow up all the big business blocks
got everyone all the adults all the kids babes animals plants
out of the way

        people singing in the streets
        bake sales all over the place

that's the same year that blackrobed judge
coughs up a whole turtle egg snap snap snap
says that turtle egg
snap snap

      change the past so's we can change the storm
      says that old lady to that turtle egg
      best hatching moon ever

there's wax and then there's wane
this is at the first annual turtle island land recognitions
pow wow trail
thousands of miles and hundreds of bands
and billions of dollars raised
on account of all the kids with tb asthma diabetes
all the elders
take a stand
biggest crowds you could imagine

they say when that old lady was just a girl
her heart is so light there's a floating glowing coming
east reaches up her arms and meets the day
it's after that she has the goodness
is what the auntys say

the goodness surrounds her is her
no one no woman
not even a stuffed doll could touch or say
to face their demons
eyes and ears that see and hear their own images their own
    tones
feelings longings rememberings

where words are rare redyellow clay
soft and serious
fast-talking silence stills the pain
to hear the feel
to feel the hear
eyes full with life and love and
round brown ground

SHARRON PROULX-TURNER is a Métis writer who holds a Masters in English, Feminist Bio-theory, from the University of Calgary, and has taught at Old Sun and Mount Royal Colleges. She grew to young adulthood in the Ottawa River valley and now lives in Calgary. She is mother to Graham, Barb and Adrian. A previously published memoir was shortlisted for the Edna Staebler Award for Creative Non-Fiction. *what the auntys say* is her first book of poetry, and the culmination of years of rumination on her roots and on the power of language.